HOME BUYING AND A GLOBAL PANDEMIC

GARRICK WERDMULLER

Home Buying and a Global Pandemic

CONTENTS

INTRODUCTION

ANAHEIM

Where were you when the pandemic hit?

This is one of those questions, like 9/11, where you will remember forever where you were, who you were with, and what you were doing as news of this coronavirus hit mainstream media in 2020.

Me, I was in Anaheim at a marketing event on March 5, 2020, when it was really sinking in that I needed to GET HOME! Before leaving to fly to Anaheim, news of this virus had really just started to hit mainstream media, and they had just parked a cruise ship in the middle of the San Francisco Bay to quarantine for two weeks. (Later, that cruise ship sat haunted in the Bay for weeks, but that's a different story for a different book.) I remember a REALTOR® friend was holding a broker open house the day before I was leaving, and I stopped in to hang out with his invitation, and it was the first time I "elbow bumped."

We did a Facebook Live video, and mortgage rates were at 2.875% or below for the first time in history. I was thinking to myself, A): Why am I here? I need to be locking loans. B): Why am I not leaving? I should be locking loans. And C): Can someone please explain what is happening here?

It was literally unfathomable the amount of business that got thrown in the face of every loan officer in March of 2020 as I flew into Anaheim, went to the event, and I am glad I did. I saw a lot of friends in the business whom I hadn't seen in years, and what I didn't know then was that I wouldn't see them for quite some time to come. It was one of the last corporate events the hotel had. I was down the street from Disneyland, where I was six weeks earlier for my birthday. Ironically, people were fleeing Disneyland, and soon it would close for the rest of the year and into 2021. (I was one of the only people that went to Disneyland in 2020... unfathomable at the time and still is!) At this time, I saw China's manufacturing statistics, and China had basically closed all manufacturing. Again, unfathomable. Meanwhile, rates were insanely low. I remember the night of the event. I was going to work all night in my room and ended up going out to dinner. As I passed a friend on the way to the elevator, he said, "That steak is going to cost you 80 grand!" He was laughing because it was so busy, and rates were rapidly going up the day of the event.

The next day I found myself inside my hotel room, working and waiting for my flight. When I got home, I swear I had never taken a longer, hotter shower. I instantly just dumped the clothes out of my suitcase into the washing machine, ran it on hot, and bagged my dry cleaning.

After that, the schools closed. There was no more toilet paper anywhere, and we were trapped in our homes, working and homeschooling... unfathomable. (Have I used that word yet?) We thought it would be six weeks, then, until the fall, but the world would be changed for a very long-time, friends, and that is where our story begins...

So, if you want to buy a house, this book will educate you on what went down at the beginning of the pandemic to change the lending industry indefinitely, how the real estate industry changed, and what you need to do to win in this market.

CHAPTER 1

MARCH 2020 IN A NUTSHELL

Many of you may be reading this book looking for information to help navigate you through the home-buying process in a world post-COVID-19. Whether you are a new home buyer or a seasoned real estate investor, the process can certainly be a bit challenging to traverse under normal circumstances. Add in a global pandemic, and even veteran real estate experts are being turned upside down by these unprecedented times.

The good news is that the picture has become clearer on safely buying and selling real estate today. One of the many ways in which we can understand these current processes in place, as well as the current state of real estate markets, is by deconstructing where they were and analyzing the drivers that led up to the real estate environment as we now know it.

THE TIPPING POINT

The first part of 2020 started off fairly strong. Real estate prices were relatively level, and rental markets appeared robust and were gaining traction. Yet, lingering concerns about a new virus classified as COVID-19 spread quickly.

Up until March, the real estate and mortgage markets continued to see steady growth. It appeared to be business as usual; the home-ownership rate seemed to be climbing slightly or, at the very least, remained stable.

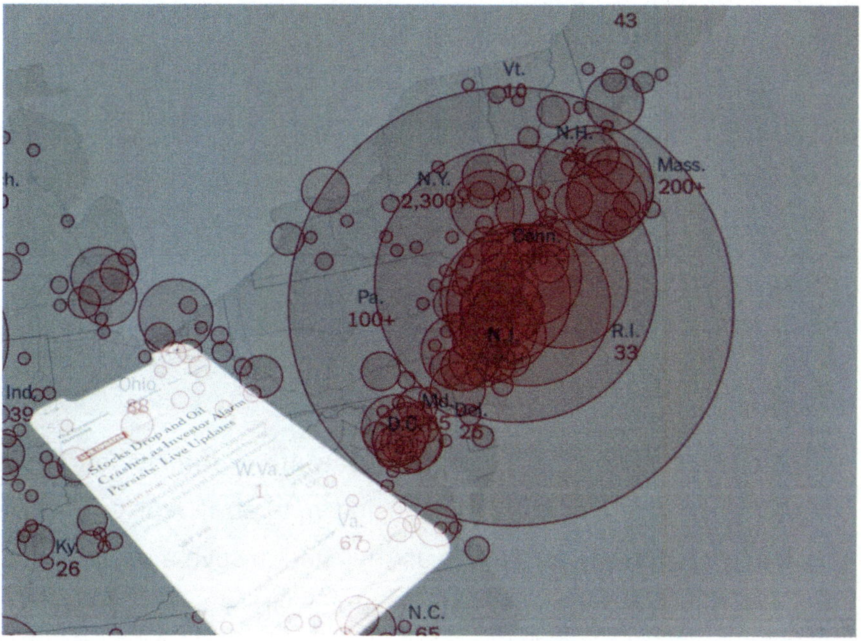

Fast forward to the middle of March, and the World Health Organization (WHO) had already issued a public health emergency warning in response to the exponential increase in the number of positive cases globally[1].

In mid- to late 2019, mortgage rates had hit an inflection point and were gradually leveling out, but by March, they began a downward trajectory[2]. The average 30-year fixed-rate mortgage hovered around 3.00%. Everything seemed favorable. It was business as usual[2].

It wasn't until March 13, 2020, that the market took a turn and seemed to be truly rattled for the first time. President Trump issued a national emergency in response to the coronavirus pandemic, which subsequently unlocked billions in federal funding to help combat the encroaching virus[1].

Financial markets began reacting with hyper-volatility as uncertainty and speculation loomed over the U.S. economy. Much like other markets, mortgage rates spiked. Businesses began closing, stay-at-home orders went into effect, and mortgage rates began to climb.

THE WHITE KNIGHT RIDES AGAIN

Alarm bells went off as analysts became extremely concerned about the solvency of the U.S. housing market. If mortgage rates continued to increase as sharply as they had in such a short period, the availability of credit could dry up along with a sizable downward shift in home prices.

Mortgage rates can indirectly impact home prices. One way to combat rising rates is by improving available inventory, thereby decreasing competition in the market[3]. The problem was that demand was already high and inventory low.

Similarly, while stronger economies—typically those with growing wages—can absorb the impacts of rate changes, it is easier to do so over longer periods[3]. The market's response warranted swift action.

Much like in response to the 2007-2008 financial crisis, the Federal Reserve instituted immediate relief by slashing the benchmark interest rate and bolstering confidence amidst turbulent economic headwinds. This was the first emergency action the Fed had taken since 2008 with unanimous consent almost two weeks before its regularly scheduled meeting[4].

While cutting rates did provide a lifeline to mortgage and real estate markets, there were still evolving problems that required immediate answers. Slashing rates could not stop businesses from hemorrhaging, borrowers from losing their jobs, or reduce the number of positive cases.

Additionally, the quick response had a whiplash reactionary effect in the market. Suddenly, lenders and borrowers alike could no longer be certain about the trajectory of mortgage rates or even the housing market as a whole.

Most importantly, it didn't address the growing liquidity crisis that followed the passing of the Coronavirus Aid, Relief, and Economic Security (CARES) Act later that month.

For loan originators, we were inundated with calls immediately. The general public thought that mortgage rates went to zero percent with a Fed Rate cut to zero percent. Mortgage rates and the Federal Funds rate are two completely separate animals, and mortgage rates were hovering around 4% at the time. I discuss mortgage and Fed Funds rates in this video: https://www.youtube.com/watch?v=ZxwOZRSDQFM if you want to know more.

NO OPTIONS FOR NON-QM

In a time when non-QM or non-qualified mortgages were becoming increasingly popular, especially with real estate investors, self-employed borrowers, and borrowers with non-traditional income sources, the coronavirus pandemic created major setbacks to the point where the majority of non-QM providers had to cease originating new loans completely.

Non-QM mortgages often have the upside of offering more flexible credit and financial requirements compared to those of traditional mortgage products. Since they do not have to adhere to the lending standards set forth by the Dodd-Frank Act, they can take a more proprietary approach to risk.

But as economic uncertainty ran rampant, investors' appetite for the enhanced risk associated with many non-QM solutions dried up. The number of providers took a nosedive to the point where almost all non-QM lending ceased. QM lending even became muted to a point, as the focus on analyzing a borrower's ability to repay became a clouded process.

The same held true for jumbo mortgage providers. Jumbo mortgages are loans that exceed the conventional conforming loan parameters set forth by the Federal Housing Finance Agency (FHFA). Because these loans could not be guaranteed by Fannie Mae or Freddie Mac, much like other non-QM solutions, they are not awarded the same protections in the event of borrower default.

As a result, borrowers turned to hard money or private lenders to satisfy their lending needs. The problem is that hard money lenders often require larger down payments, additional documented reserves, and charge higher interest rates to cushion against added risk.

I started 2020 with two big presentations on non-QM loans for REALTORs®. They loved it, and they went over great. Then in one day, the market was GONE! The last time I saw something dry up like that was 2007/2008 when Washington Mutual, among others, were no longer doing the "No Doc," but this was in one or two days for non-QM.

A DOUBLE-EDGED SWORD

As a response to the economic fallout brought about by COVID-19, the federal government quickly passed the largest stimulus package recorded in American history. The Coronavirus Aid, Relief, and Economic Security (CARES) Act was a $2.2 trillion relief package that greatly boosted solvency for households and businesses nationwide[1].

One of the most significant impacts to the housing market was that individuals affected by COVID-19 that requested and received payment flexibility from creditors were still required to be reported as compliant with their payments.

Similarly, households with federally backed mortgages were protected from foreclosure through the end of August 20205. Borrowers could also request forbearance for up to 180 days, after which they could request an extension where warranted[5].

But the immediate relief that home owners found from this piece of legislation came with an opposite downward swing from the pendulum. Suddenly, as 3 million or more Americans took advantage of the granted forbearance provision, mortgage servicers experienced a liquidity crisis[6].

Servicers had to advance the funds for the uncollected payments that borrowers didn't make under the CARES Act to cover forbearance plans to bondholders. However, this was difficult because servicers were also burdened with maintaining stringent capitalization requirements.

While the front-end benefits of the CARES Act did provide short-term assistance to borrowers, backed-end markets struggled to maintain solvency. The other issue that was simultaneously brewing was ensuring that the loans investors were selling into the secondary market were up to par with industry standards. I have a summary of how it all went down from this interview I did for an event, Navigate the Lockdown: https://www.youtube.com/watch?v=wlOxGECxGSA.

PILE ON THE PAPERWORK

Many large lenders' appetite for risk decreased dramatically as a direct response to various factors in the market. This resulted in many lenders broadly tightening credit eligibility requirements on new mortgage loans.

A few weeks after the CARES Act went into effect, JPMorgan Chase announced a new policy stipulating that borrowers trying to attain a new mortgage would need a FICO credit score of at least 700 while also requiring a minimum down payment for new purchases of at least 20%[7]. U.S. Bank and Wells Fargo quickly followed suit by also raising the borrowing standards for new mortgage originations[8].

In many ways, these new policies grew as a direct response to concerns about the number of borrowers seeking forbearance relief. The problem was that tightening standards meant American families were almost implicitly forced to choose between utilizing a loss-mitigation solution or forgoing the option for a possibility at buying or refinancing.

If your credit report showed your mortgage was currently in forbearance or a deferred status, then there were consequently new hoops you had to jump through to become eligible for a new mortgage.

In addition to lenders adopting new internal credit eligibility requirements, implementing multiple temporary investor overlays and guidance also impacted the mortgage qualification process.

Fannie Mae and Freddie Mac both announced the adoption of new "flexibilities" geared toward helping maintain the credit quality of mortgage loans being purchased in the secondary market.

An example includes increased documentation and due diligence for self-employed borrowers. Borrowers who owned and operated businesses now had to prove their solvency by showing additional asset statements, proof of activity (i.e., invoices, sales receipts, scheduled appointments, etc.), as well as YTD profit and loss statements9. If the stability and continuance of the business cash flows were called into question, even more documentation would be required, or, in some cases, the income couldn't be used for qualification at all[9].

New employment verification rules were also adopted to verify that borrowers were still employed, and that income was still expected to continue upon funding any new mortgage loan[10]. New business verifications also went into effect, and most lenders now required all borrowers to affirm their financial status, attesting that they foresaw nor expected any immediate changes to their income or intended to apply for forbearance soon after obtaining a new mortgage loan[10].

Another area of concern was the collateral being used to back new mortgage loans. Typically, standard practice would be for lenders to order an appraisal report to verify the property's value supported the loan request. But many borrowers and appraisers felt it a risk to do formal on-site inspections for fear of contracting the virus. There was also a general lack of appraisers, and those who were still active were often in an aging, higher risk group. Those appraisers willing to take assignments began charging more for riskier inspections, such as investment properties with multiple tenants.

Other relevant investor overlays included a tightening of age requirements with respect to documentation being collected and submitted with any given mortgage application. Pre-COVID-19 standards allowed for a multitude of documents to be no more than 120 days old at delivery; however, the new rules cut this requirement in half for most documents, now down to 60 days.

Furthermore, updated mortgage statements and the use of credit supplements also became fundamental ways lenders could verify a borrower's existing mortgage was paid and current.

New COVID-19 overlays seemed to impact multiple groups: borrowers had to meet higher credit standards, lenders required more documentation and saw a sizable increase in turn times, and investors saw quality control issues with loans being delivered into the secondary market. It's fair to say all processes became much less palatable.

A great thing about being a broker in this period was that WE excelled thanks to a free marketplace and the ability to go to more solvent lenders. We could also see which lenders were imploding due to volume and avoid those as much as possible.

SOURCES

1 AJMC. (2021, January 02). A Timeline of COVID-19 Developments in 2020. Retrieved February 23, 2021, from https://www.ajmc.com/view/a-timeline-of-covid19-developments-in-2020

2 Freddie Mac. (2021, February 18). Current Mortgage Rates Data Since 1971. Retrieved February 23, 2021, from http://www.freddiemac.com/pmms/

3 Campisi, N. (2018, April 10). Do Rising Mortgage Rates Trigger Lower House Prices? Retrieved February 23, 2021, from https://www.bankrate.com/finance/mortgages/rising-rates-lower-house-prices.aspx

4 Long, H. (2020, March 16). Federal Reserve slashes interest rates to zero as part of wide-ranging emergency intervention. Retrieved February 23, 2021, from https://www.washingtonpost.com/business/2020/03/15/federal-reserve-slashes-interest-rates-zero-part-wide-ranging-emergency-intervention/

5 Consumer Financial Protection Bureau. (n.d.). CARES Act Mortgage Forbearance: What You Need to Know. Retrieved February 23, 2021, from https://www.consumerfinance.gov/coronavirus/mortgage-and-housing-assistance/cares-act-mortgage-forbearance-what-you-need-know/

6 DianaOlick. (2020, April 21). As mortgage bailout balloons amid coronavirus outbreak, servicers finally get some relief. Retrieved February 23, 2021, from https://www.cnbc.com/2020/04/21/coronavirus-as-mortgage-bailout-balloons-servicers-finally-get-some-relief.html

7 JPMorgan Chase to raise mortgage borrowing standards as economic outlook darkens. (2020, April 13). Retrieved February 23,

2021, from https://www.cnbc.com/2020/04/11/jpmorgan-chase-to-raise-mortgage-borrowing-standards-as-economic-outlook-darkens.

8 Campisi, N. (2020, April 14). Mortgage Borrowers Face Stricter Rules In Coronavirus Pullback. Retrieved February 23, 2021, from https://www.bankrate.com/mortgages/requirements-tighten-with-coronavirus-job-losses/

9 Freddie Mac. (2020, November 13). Selling Guidance Related to COVID-19 (This is a reissuance of Bulletin 2020-44 made on November 13, 2020). Retrieved February 23, 2021, from https://guide.freddiemac.com/app/guide/bulletin/2020-44

10 https://guide.freddiemac.com/app/guide/section/5302.2

CHAPTER 2

BANKS, BROKERS, AND ROCKETS, OH MY! WHERE DO I GO TO GET A LOAN?

Contrary to popular belief, not all lenders are created equal! You have several options when buying a home, starting with choosing which lender you want to work with.

Some lenders are completely flexible and offer a full range of mortgage financing solutions, while others are more niche, providing only a handful of mortgage products for you to choose from.

Finding the right lender can help dictate the sort of buying experience you have, whether you want a more streamlined digital explicitly digital experience or a lender with multiple options that can address your specific financing situation.

Here are some of the more common mortgage providers you may want to consider:

Mortgage Brokers

A mortgage broker is usually a local independent intermediary who brings mortgage borrowers and mortgage lenders together but who does not use their own funds to originate mortgages. A mortgage broker helps borrowers connect with lenders and seeks out the best fit for the borrower's financial situation and interest-rate needs. The mortgage broker also gathers paperwork from the borrower and passes that paperwork along to a mortgage lender for underwriting and approval. The broker earns a commission from either the borrower, the lender, or both at closing.

National "Big" Banks

National banks are the "too big to fail" institutions we all know that offer a full spectrum of banking products including, but not limited to, personal and business deposit accounts, home loans, commercial loans, consumer loans, equity lines of credit, retirement accounts, and more.

Mortgage Banks

A mortgage bank is a bank that specializes in originating and/or servicing mortgage loans. In the U.S., a mortgage bank is a state-licensed banking entity that makes mortgage loans directly to consumers. The difference between a mortgage banker and a mortgage broker is that the mortgage banker funds loans with its own capital.

Credit Unions

A credit union is a member-owned financial cooperative, controlled by its members and operated on the principle of people helping people, providing its members with credit at competitive rates alongside other financial services.

Online or Digital Lenders

The term "online mortgage" refers to a mortgage from a lender with no physical presence. The exact process varies depending on the lender. But in general, an online mortgage should allow you to accomplish key tasks like getting rate quotes, filling out an application, and providing documents without having to sit down with a loan officer. In some cases, you may not even need to dig up all the documents yourself.

In-House Construction Lender

In the real estate industry, most home builders will use an in-house lender and often offer buyer incentives by processing the loan through their own mortgage company. In-house mortgage companies are sometimes scrutinized by other mortgage companies because outside or third-party mortgage companies cannot compete with their internal market rates or discount the lending incentives that the builder offers.

In-House Real Estate Lender

An in-house lender is generally someone who sits in the real estate agent's office to field questions and offer loan programs and advice to the agent's clients. The real estate brokerage earns a desk fee or has an ownership interest in the corporation set up between the real estate brokerage and the mortgage bank.

TYPES OF MORTGAGE LOANS

After you figure out who the perfect broker or lender is that you want to partner with for buying your next home, the next step is to narrow in exactly what type of mortgage financing you want to utilize for your purchase.

Much like mortgage providers, there are numerous mortgage solutions to choose from. Some may be more advantageous than others, depending on your specific situation and background. While you may want to lean on your mortgage broker or loan officer for guidance, it's also worthwhile to have a general idea of the different mortgage programs available.

Here are some of the more common types of mortgage loans that may be readily available:

Conventional Mortgages

Most traditional mortgage loans are referred to as conventional mortgages. This type of mortgage is usually conforming, meaning it meets the guidelines to be purchased by aggregators Fannie Mae or Freddie Mac, but it can also be non-conforming[2]. Ultimately, it is not guaranteed or insured by the federal government, subsequently requiring stricter credit requirements than most government-sponsored programs. Transactions with less than 20% down will also usually require cancellable private mortgage insurance[3].

Benefits: Most common type of mortgage, typically faster underwriting, cancellable private mortgage insurance, affordable lending options available

Government-Sponsored Mortgage Programs

FHA Mortgages. Notorious for having some of the most flexible qualifying credit requirements, an FHA mortgage is insured by the Federal Housing Administration (FHA). They are designed for low-to-moderate-income borrowers and often require lower minimum down payments and credit scores. With an FHA mortgage, you may be required to pay mortgage insurance premiums.

Benefits: More liberal credit eligibility requirements, sellers can pay a portion of closing costs

VA Mortgages. If you are an eligible service member, veteran, or surviving spouse of someone in the U.S. armed forces, you may qualify for a VA mortgage. Much like FHA mortgages, VA mortgages are insured by the U.S. Department of Veterans Affairs and can offer some of the most competitive interest rates and down payment requirements without necessarily requiring mortgage insurance.

Benefits: No down payment options, no prepayment penalties, funding fee vs. PMI/MIPs

USDA Mortgages. Championed for being one of the most popular mortgage solutions that can offer qualified borrowers a no down payment option, USDA mortgages are another federally insured mortgage solution. These loans are backed by the U.S. Department of Agriculture (USDA). Income-driven and geared more toward underserved rural areas, USDA mortgages offer a variety of flexibility, including permitting large acreage sites[4], as well as manufactured and modular homes.

Benefits: Max loan amount up to 100% of subject appraised value, not limited to first-time home buyers

Non-QM Mortgage Programs

Non-QM Mortgage. You may hear mortgage providers use the term "non-QM" as industry jargon to refer to a mortgage that is not considered a "qualified mortgage." A qualified mortgage is a mortgage that meets certain borrower and lender parameters as outlined by the Consumer Financial Protection Bureau and Dodd-Frank Act[5]. Non-QM mortgages often have more flexibility when analyzing a borrower's ability to repay, making them popular among borrowers that have non-traditional income sources or are self-employed.

Benefits: More relaxed credit requirements, options for non-traditional borrowers

Jumbo Mortgage. Jumbo mortgages are the quintessential example of a non-QM mortgage. Their key characteristic is that they carry a loan amount that exceeds the current conforming loan limits. Jumbo loans can be conventional loans, typically carry a higher interest rate than conforming mortgages, and are generally used to finance high-end or luxury real estate6.

Benefits: Loan limits exceeding the set conforming thresholds, typically no private mortgage insurance requirements

Foreign National Mortgage. Qualifying international borrowers, non-U.S. citizens, and non-permanent resident aliens can use a foreign national mortgage as an option to purchase real estate in the United States[7]. They can be used to finance investment real estate as well as a new primary dwelling. Typically, these loans are subject to higher down payment requirements and may also require additional verified reserves and an international credit report. Many programs offer fixed-rate as well as adjustable-rate options.

Benefits: Potential tax benefits, diversification, and the ability to purchase higher value property

Other Mortgage Programs

Hard Money Mortgages. Hard money mortgages are often offered by independent private individuals or organizations focusing mainly on the underlying collateral asset above most other things when making a loan decision. Often epitomized as being more expensive, hard money mortgages charge a premium for the added non-traditional transaction risk but have a reputation for being a quick financing, short-term option when needed.

Benefits: Less concerned about poor credit, application and underwriting process is often quick

Home Equity Loan or Line of Credit. Often referred to as second mortgages (although they are not restricted to only being in the second lien position), home equity loans and lines of credit

are another type of mortgage borrowers can obtain[8]. Home equity loans are typically for a fixed loan amount and come with a fixed term, while home equity lines of credit are revolving loans that work similarly to credit card loans but are collateralized with your home's equity. Home equity loans and lines of credit are popular as a piggyback second mortgage, used to finance home renovations, or can help you consolidate other high-interest debt.

Benefits: Variety of different loan plans, liberal use of loan proceeds, fairly quick application process

Reverse Mortgages. Unlike a traditional mortgage, a reverse mortgage uses the available equity in your home and converts it to a lump sum or fixed monthly payments[9]. As the borrower, you do not make any monthly loan payments, but rather the lender makes one-time or regular monthly payments directly to you in exchange for an ever-increasing equity position in the home. The mortgage comes due if you sell the home, move away permanently, or pass away.

Benefits: Can create a recurring income stream, only have to cover your property's maintenance, taxes, and insurance obligations

HOW TO DECIDE: FIXED OR ADJUSTABLE?

If it wasn't enough of a challenge figuring out which lender to partner with and which mortgage loan program to choose, another feature you must decide is if you want your mortgage to be a fixed rate or adjustable. While either option works with almost all mortgage loan types, each has its own set of pros and cons.

Fixed-Rate Mortgages

Just like the name suggests, fixed-rate mortgages are set up to charge a set interest rate for the full life of the loan. This means that the rate does not change with the movement of current market prices.

Because your interest rate is fixed, there is a predictability to your monthly payment. Your overall principal and interest payment will heavily depend on your interest rate, term, and initial loan amount.

Traditionally, fixed-rate mortgages can be taken at 30-, 25-, 20-, 15-, and 10-year terms. In general, the longer your loan term, the smaller your monthly payment. However, conversely, this also means that the longer your term, the more money you will ultimately pay in interest.

While your monthly payment will remain fixed over the life of your loan, most mortgages are structured so that more of your payment goes toward interest than principal for the first few years of your term. The longer you keep making payments, the more of your payment you can expect to gradually be allocated toward your principal balance.

Adjustable-Rate Mortgages

An ARM or an adjustable-rate mortgage is in many ways similar to a fixed-rate mortgage. For example, your payments are typically lower the longer your term. However, the main caveat with adjustable-rate mortgages is that the interest rate is subject to change over time.

The Consumer Financial Protection Bureau (CFPB) highlights that with many adjustable-rate mortgages, your loan may start with a lower interest rate (sometimes referred to as a teaser rate) for the first few months or even years[1].

After this initial introductory period, your interest rate can then be subject to change based on an adjustment schedule. The adjustment schedule is a prearranged frequency of when the rate for your mortgage can adjust. In some cases, it can adjust every month, whereas in others, it can adjust every year or more.

The interest rate of your loan is tied to a benchmark index, with the most common now being the secured overnight financing rate (SOFR)[10]. Your interest rate is also determined by a set margin, typically expressed as a set percentage of your pay above the benchmark index. One example would be if the SOFR rate was 1.00% and your margin was 2.00% at the time your rate would adjust, your new effective interest rate would be 3.00% (1.00% + 2.00%).

Another point to note is that ARMs have caps and ceilings. Caps are specific limits to the number of times a rate can increase each adjustment period, while a ceiling refers to the maximum highest rate that your interest rate can adjust to over the life of your loan. There are limits to both.

Advantages and Disadvantages: Fixed vs. Adjustable

Traditionally, most borrowers gravitate toward fixed-rate mortgages because there is a level of predictability. It makes it easier to budget, and they are much easier to understand. The downside is that if rates go lower, your rate remains fixed, meaning you could potentially miss out on future savings depending on the trajectory of market rates.

On the other hand, adjustable-rate mortgages can be quite lucrative. The biggest advantage is that you can often get a cheaper rate than most fixed-rate mortgages throughout the introductory period. Furthermore, in many cases, a lower initial rate means you might be able to qualify for a larger loan amount.

However, a major disadvantage of choosing an adjustable-rate mortgage is the market volatility. If you are not prepared to weather potential market fluctuations when it comes time for your rate to adjust, you could be in a worse off position than you initially intended.

ALWAYS CONSIDER YOUR PITIA

One simple truth is that brokers, loan officers, and real estate agents alike like to throw around industry jargon expecting buyers to know exactly what they mean. While you aren't studying for a grammar school spelling test, one phrase you should know is PITIA.

Principal + Interest + Taxes + Insurance +
Association Dues and/or PMI

PITIA essentially refers to your consolidated monthly mortgage payment. Obviously, your mortgage payment consists of several things, but the two main pieces are the principal and interest portion to your payment.

The principal is the portion of your payment that goes toward the actual amount you borrowed. This is also the portion that translates into equity. In contrast, interest is the cost to borrow that money. It is the premium your lender charges for lending you the money and taking on the risk.

But while your mortgage payment could stop there, lenders also factor other expenses into your proposed monthly payment. This includes expenses such as the real estate taxes you owe based on your property's assessed value and home owner's insurance for protecting your home against a variety of events.

Lastly, do not forget about any applicable monthly assessments if you plan on buying a property in a community development or project. Your assessments could be charged annually (if so, just divide by 12) or monthly. The other expense to consider is any mortgage insurance premiums you will need to pay if you are putting down less than 20% on your new home.

To learn more about PITIA, visit https://www.consumerfinance.gov/ask-cfpb/what-is-piti-en-152/.

SOURCES

1 Consumer Financial Protection Bureau. (2017, September 25). What is the difference between a fixed-rate and adjustable-rate mortgage (ARM) loan? Retrieved March 4, 2021, from https://www.consumerfinance.gov/ask-cfpb/

what-is-the-difference-between-a-fixed-rate-and-adjustable-rate-mortgage-arm-loan-en-100/#:~:text=The difference between a fixed rate and an adjustable rate,may go up or down.&text=Some ARMs set a cap,your interest rate can go

2 Federal Housing Finance Agency. (n.d.). Conforming Loan Limits. Retrieved March 11, 2021, from https://www.fhfa.gov/DataTools/Downloads/Pages/Conforming-Loan-Limits.aspx

3 Consumer Financial Protection Bureau. (2017, July 28). What is private mortgage insurance? Retrieved March 11, 2021, from https://www.consumerfinance.gov/ask-cfpb/what-is-private-mortgage-insurance-en-122/

4 US Department of Agriculture. (2020). *Single Family Housing Guaranteed Loan Program* [Brochure]. Author. Retrieved March 11, 2021, from https://www.rd.usda.gov/sites/default/files/Guarantee_SFH_Flyer.pdf

5 Hayes, A. (2021, March 04). Dodd-Frank Definition. Retrieved March 11, 2021, from https://www.investopedia.com/terms/d/dodd-frank-financial-regulatory-reform-bill.asp

6 Investopedia. (2020, August 28). Jumbo Loan. Retrieved March 11, 2021, from https://www.investopedia.com/terms/j/jumboloan.asp#:~:text=A jumbo loan, also known,Housing Finance Agency (FHFA).&text=Designed to finance luxury properties,underwriting requirements and tax implications.

7 Pogol, G. (2020, February 19). Foreign national mortgage for non-US citizens. Retrieved March 11, 2021, from https://themortgagereports.com/26221/foreign-national-mortgage-for-non-us-citizens

8 Federal Trade Commission. (2018, March 13). Home Equity Loans and Credit Lines. Retrieved March 11, 2021, from https://www.consumer.ftc.gov/articles/0227-home-equity-loans-and-credit-lines

9 Fontinelle, A. (2021, February 23). Reverse Mortgages Definition. Retrieved March 11, 2021, from https://www.investopedia.com/mortgage/reverse-mortgage/

10 Kurt, D. (2020, December 24). Secured Overnight Financing Rate (SOFR). Retrieved March 11, 2021, from https://www.investopedia.com/secured-overnight-financing-rate-sofr-4683954

CHAPTER 3

YOU FOUND THE HOME OF YOUR DREAMS. NOW WHAT?

Ask any realtor you want to show you homes, and they will ask if you have already received a mortgage pre-approval. Thousands of new home buyers are entering the market trying to take advantage of the favorable mortgage rate environment. Sellers are becoming increasingly selective on which buyers they really want to sell to.

Consequently, getting pre-approved is now more important than ever because it means, unlike other buyers you might be competing against, that you have already taken the time to complete a mortgage application, had a lender run your credit, and have had your income and assets tentatively approved to meet credit qualification requirements.

As inventory continues to remain low, sellers have found that asking for a pre-approval letter can help weed out better, more reliable offers. Recent data indicates that most buyers purchase their home for 99% of the asking price, and 87% financed their home purchase[1]. Thus, it goes to show that having a pre-approval letter will indicate to sellers that you are a serious buyer.

Similarly, as the pandemic continues to impact the housing market, agents recommend that sellers limit tours and showings only to buyers who can demonstrate they have been pre-approved for financing[2].

While it may sound like a lot of extra work, getting pre-approved has never been easier. Let's take a closer look at the steps you and your broker will work through together to help get you pre-approved and into that new dream home!

PREQUALIFIED VERSUS PREAPPROVED: WHAT'S THE DIFFERENCE?

Making the leap to getting pre-approved is one of the first steps to home ownership. The next step is figuring out which type of pre-approval is best suited for you. Contrary to popular belief, there

are a few different ways to become pre-approved, all with varying measures of weight that they carry to the table.

Prequalification

The most basic form of being pre-approved is actually more commonly referred to as a pre-qualification. While pre-qualifications and pre-approvals are often used interchangeably, they are not exactly the same thing.

Ultimately, a pre-qualification carries far less weight than a formal pre-approval. That's because, with a pre-qualification, you are only providing a few pieces of data to a lender who provides you with a ballpark estimate of what you can probably afford (the key word being "probably")[3].

While getting a pre-qualification, on the surface, seems better than having no form of pre-approval at all, note that the lender has completed no due diligence to determine if you really have a strong likelihood at qualifying for a new mortgage loan.

Preapproved

In contrast, a formal mortgage pre-approval involves a much more thorough investigation of your credit, income, and financial assets[3]. Typically, you will need to fill out a formal application and provide your broker with your income documentation and bank statements. They will also complete a formal credit check to verify your credit history, outstanding debts, and credit score.

Getting pre-approved involves a heavier vetting process, which is why sellers place more weight on an actual pre-approval letter over a simple pre-qualification.

Another benefit to going with a full pre-approval is that it usually satisfies a lot of the application process up front, meaning potentially less documentation to provide later on when your mortgage goes to underwriting (depending on how long it takes you to find a home). Keep in mind that depending on your lender, pre-approvals are usually good for 60–90 days on average[3].

Certified Home Buyer

Most borrowers typically go with a pre-approval, start shopping for their forever home, and call it a day. But most buyers don't realize there is a third pre-approval option that blows a normal pre-approval out of the water: becoming a certified home buyer[3].

Sometimes referred to as a fully underwritten pre-approval, a certified home buyer is one that goes through all the typical steps to become pre-approved but takes it a step further by actually submitting their file to a mortgage underwriter.

Here, your application will be fully reviewed and scrutinized for eligibility. The underwriting process is very detail-oriented and notorious for being long. However, the benefit is that you will have more confidence knowing you qualify for that new mortgage.

Additionally, you will also get peace of mind knowing an underwriter has scrutinized and corrected any errors, which can save you time and money with issues coming up at the last minute.

Finally, becoming a certified home buyer will make you a much more attractive buyer over others that are simply pre-approved. This is especially relevant when there are multiple offers on the table[3].

Ultimately, make sure you stand out by starting the process early and obtaining some sort of pre-approval, whether that be a pre-qualification or working to become a certified home buyer. Discuss the pros and cons with your preferred mortgage broker.

UNDERSTANDING WHAT YOU CAN AFFORD

If you start overthinking the home-buying process, it can be very easy to become overwhelmed. That's why it's best to start with clear expectations about the type of home you want and how much you can afford.

Figuring out how much home you can afford will help set a nice foundation for a smooth and successful purchase. That is why it is important to start the conversation with a preferred mortgage broker.

Working as your partner and advocate, your mortgage broker will help you balance your current housing needs with your budget, discussing different financing solutions with you along the way. In some cases, using one of the many free affordability calculators available can analyze the maximum purchase price your budget can truly handle.

But understanding affordability doesn't stop there. Knowing what documentation your lender will be requesting and what data they will be analyzing throughout the credit approval process will help streamline the mortgage application process.

Here are a few things that your lender will be looking at when qualifying you for a new mortgage loan. This is referred to as the three-legged stool of getting pre-approved. You need these three legs to be equally strong.

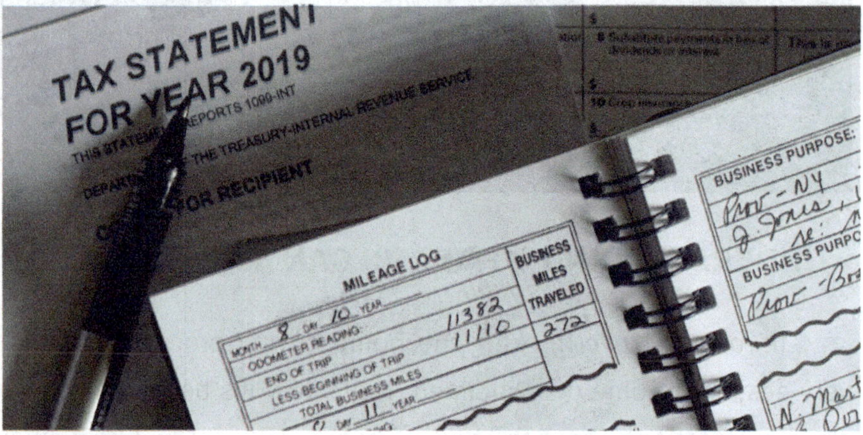

Leg 1: Your Credit

Probably one of the most confusing topics out there, no matter what kind of loan you are applying for, analyzing your credit involves dissecting your credit score and your overall credit history and utilization as a measure of risk.

According to credit repository Experian, five key factors go into your credit report: your payment history, your credit usage (or the amount of debt that you owe), your credit history length, your credit mix, and new credit accounts that you have opened[4].

Keep in mind that your payment history and credit utilization account for 65% of your overall FICO score, which is the score used by most mortgage providers[4]. Sam Parker, CEO of MyCreditGuy, also notes that you will want to get your score up to around 740 to get the best rate and pricing for most mortgage loans. (You can see a video with credit tips from Sam Parker and me here: https://www.youtube.com/watch?v=E-gBums1dHk&list=PL6vQsDlfZQak2ZP1scjgv8dnZnxVNFQiy&index=26)

If you have had a mortgage loan previously, it's also important to note that due to the COVID-19 pandemic, many lenders have become hyper-vigilant about verifying your current payment history. You may be asked to prove that your existing mortgage is both paid and current. Loans in forbearance or that are currently deferred are potential red flags and can gum up the approval process.

Leg 2: Your Income

Obviously, you can't qualify for a loan if you have no means to repay it. Verifying your employment history and income used to repay your new mortgage is all part of the qualification process.

If you are a traditional wage earner, most employers will require a two-year work history along with 30 days' worth of pay stubs and your most recent W-2.

If you are self-employed, be prepared to provide even more documentation as lenders scrutinize the stability and likelihood of your business being able to distribute earnings to you for the purposes of repayment.

Here is a non-exhaustive list of items your lender will most likely need to analyze your income:

- Two years of personal and business tax returns (with all schedules and worksheets)
- An unaudited signed and dated year-to-date profit and loss statement and balance sheet
- Three months of business bank statements (showing deposits and/or reserves)
- Proof of business activity (i.e., set appointments, business invoices, receivables, etc.)

Leg 3: Your Assets

Equally important to your eligibility is verifying that you have enough money actually to purchase your new home. Lenders must verify your assets to determine if you have enough funds to cover your down payment and closing costs.

For some transactions, you may also need to provide assets to show you have funds in reserves to cover your mortgage payment over 2–8 months.

Ultimately, be prepared to provide two or even three months of asset statements. You should also document and provide a paper trail for any large deposits that are not payroll-related. Make sure your name, institution, statement date, and last four digits of your account number are listed.

SOURCES

1 Highlights From the Profile of Home Buyers and Sellers. (2020, March 05). Retrieved March 11, 2021, from https://www.nar.realtor/research-and-statistics/research-reports/highlights-from-the-profile-of-home-buyers-and-sellers#home%20buyers

2 Should Preapproval Letters Be Required For Home Tours? (2020, July 08). Realtor Magazine. Retrieved March 11, 2021, from https://magazine.realtor/daily-news/2020/07/08/should-preapproval-letters-be-required-for-home-tours

3 Ramsey Solutions. (2019, June 17). Mortgage Preapproval vs. Prequalification: What's the Difference? Retrieved March 11, 2021, from https://www.daveramsey.com/blog/mortage-prequalification-vs-preapproval

4 Experian Information Solutions, Inc. (2021, January 20). What Affects Your Credit Scores? Retrieved March 11, 2021, from https://www.experian.com/blogs/ask-experian/credit-education/score-basics/what-affects-your-credit-scores/

CHAPTER 4

HOME-BUYING, OPEN HOUSES, AND WRITING OFFERS DURING A GLOBAL PANDEMIC

As I mentioned, mortgage markets were going crazy from the fallout of COVID-19; phones were ringing off the hook. With the Fed's announcement that it was slashing rates to 0%, home owners thought mortgage rates were actually at zero. In actuality, rates still sat around 4% and the news about rates consequently nearly halted real estate sales completely.

With the general ambiguity of what direction real estate markets were headed in, what processes needed to change to conduct business safely, and how industry professionals could bolster consumer confidence in the market again, many agents fell on hard times.

According to the Washington Post, over 10 million Americans applied for unemployment benefits in the wake of March 2020[1].

Realtors contributed to these numbers as the newly enacted CARES Act broadened the eligibility of citizens to apply for benefits.

Sales activity took an initial nosedive, and open houses and broker's tours were canceled indefinitely. Buyers were no longer permitted to enter sellers' homes, and, conversely, sellers didn't want them there for fear of exposure.

That said, the market had seen some tremendous growth during the latter half of 2020. While the real estate and mortgage industries have both been notoriously slow to keep pace with a world becoming increasingly digitized, new processes and tools have become available to both buyers and sellers that can help streamline the sales process while maintaining the health of all parties involved.

Let us take a look at how the home-buying process has evolved since the pandemic began, how open houses and tours are now being handled, and how you can write an offer guaranteed to be accepted over all others.

CHANGES TO THE HOME-BUYING PROCESS

In many ways, aspects of the home-buying process have already evolved toward incorporating more electronic and digital processes. However, the pandemic certainly accelerated these transitions, effectively forcing all parties involved in each real estate transaction to adopt new ways of doing business.

It should be noted that one of the biggest drivers for change has been newer generations of home buyers entering the market. The latest generational report published by the National Association of Realtors notes that buyers between the ages of 22 and 39 (Millennials and Gen Y-ers) made up 38% of all home buyers, with over half of this segment being first-time home buyers[2].

But what's surprising is that 52% of all buyers (not just younger generations) found the home they purchased online2. Research has found that about 25% of all shoppers would buy a home without ever walking through it[3].

Virtual, Video, and 3D Tours

While that may sound crazy, new technologies have actually helped make the buying and sales process a bit easier—an almost silver lining amidst the global health crisis.

If you are looking to buy a home but are concerned about exposure, there are now multiple ways to take a personalized tour without leaving the comfort of your living room. Video tours have become extremely popular; in fact, Zillow recently showed a 191% jump in the number of 3D home tours created for various properties[3].

If you want a fully immersive experience, consider having a realtor video chat the entire thing or even just selective features for any given property you might be interested in purchasing. According to Realtor.com, nearly 44% of sellers stated they would let an agent walk a buyer through their home via video chat[3].

Appraisal and Property Inspection Waivers (PIW)

If you have ever purchased a home, you might know that obtaining a new mortgage is one of the longest parts of the entire transaction. That is because your underwriter will want to underwrite your given loan application for risk, part of which is analyzing the collateral (in this case, the home) for safety, soundness, and value.

But as aggregators Fannie Mae and Freddie Mac have compiled property data over the last decade or more, they have been transitioning to implementing big data and machine learning to the collateral analysis for new mortgage loans.

With so much more information at hand, both Fannie Mae and Freddie Mac have integrated their automated underwriting systems so that for certain files, you will no longer be required to obtain an appraisal based on the value your lender submitted for the property.

Property inspection waivers are granted on a case-by-case basis, typically for lower-risk transactions (i.e., properties with lower loan-to-value ratios, multiple borrowers, borrowers with lower DTI and high credit scores, etc.)[8].

These waivers not only limit the number of people parading through your potentially new home, but they can also help you close faster and save you more money by waiving the requirement for an appraisal altogether.

E-Sign and Digital Closings

But tours are not the only way things are changing about the home-buying process. Lenders and realtors alike have all begun adopting no-contact ways of signing documents and disclosures digitally.

While this technology is hardly anything new, what has changed is the number of providers adopting it. DocuSign, DocMagic, and DigiSigner are just a few of the electronic signature solutions that mortgage and real estate providers can use to streamline the overall buying experience.

Furthermore, the industry saw a staggering increase in the number of digital closings or eClosings in the latter part of 2020 and beyond. There are three primary types of digital closings: hybrid closings, electronic closings, and remote online closings.

Hybrid closings incorporate a mix of both electronic and traditional processes. All parties are still required to appear in person, but some documents are eSigned and eNotarized, while others require physical wet signatures[4].

For electronic closings, the same holds true that all parties appear in person. However, unlike hybrid closings, all documents are digitally signed and notarized[4].

The last and probably safest digital closing solution is a remote online closing. Using this option, all parties will eSign and eNotarize the documents via video conferencing, meaning no one needs to be in the same room[4].

While remote closings are not available in all states, title companies are getting creative with respect to socially distant options.

Curb service and drive-through closings have become extremely popular in some states to allow for safer closing protocols[5].

Lastly, a power of attorney is another unique alternative to physical closings, enabling a designated agent to physically attend and sign on your behalf.

OPEN HOUSES

If you are at all concerned about buying a home without ever having physically seen it, you are not alone. While some buyers are leaning into the fully digital home-buying experience, others are still skeptical and a little wary of buying a home without ever performing an initial walkthrough.

Before COVID-19, open houses provided an opportunity for potential buyers to view a new home (often fully furnished and decorated) before committing to an offer. But as of July 2020, walk-in open houses became strictly prohibited[6].

The Department of Public Health and Cal/OSHA have specific guidance with respect to real estate showings. For example, all showings require an appointment or a digital sign-in process prior to entry6. This may include you completing a PEAD-V form.

CALIFORNIA ASSOCIATION OF REALTORS®

CORONAVIRUS PROPERTY ENTRY ADVISORY AND DECLARATION
(C.A.R. Form PEAD, 4/20)

Property Address ______________________ Date ________

1. **RISKS OF EXPOSURE:** The Coronavirus (COVID-19) pandemic is a worldwide risk to human health. COVID-19 is highly contagious and has a mortality rate many times greater than the flu. COVID-19 can spread easily and exponentially. While people of all ages are at risk of catching COVID-19, persons especially at risk are those with compromised immune systems and the elderly. Persons over 65 years of age may be at particular risk.
2. **"STAY HOME ORDERS":** In order to reduce the spread of COVID-19, the State of California, as well as many California cities and counties have issued "Safer at Home" or "Shelter in Place" orders, with exceptions for essential activities.
3. **REAL ESTATE SALES ACTIVITIES AS ESSENTIAL SERVICES:** Under Federal and State guidelines, activities required to facilitate a real estate transaction have been deemed essential activities. Nevertheless, designation of some real estate activities as essential activities does not make them free from COVID-19 risks. All persons must still practice "social distancing" and take all steps necessary to protect themselves and others. Finally, some county and city orders are more restrictive than Federal and State guidelines and may take precedence over Federal and State guidelines.
4. **REPRESENTATION AND AGREEMENT:** By signing below, you make the following representations and agree as follows:
   A. You are either:
      (1) The seller, landlord, tenant, or occupant, voluntarily allowing someone to enter the Property for viewing, walk-through, inspections, or otherwise facilitating the real estate transaction; or
      (2) A prospective or actual buyer, tenant, real estate agent, or other person whose services facilitate the completion of a real estate transaction and are voluntarily entering the Property for the purpose of viewing, inspecting, or performing an activity or providing services in furtherance of a real estate transaction.
   B. You understand that showing and visiting properties may be dangerous or unsafe and could expose you or others to COVID-19.
   C. If applicable, you understand that your showing or visiting activities are part of an exception to Federal and State "Safer at Home" or "Shelter in Place" orders and that you are conducting those activities at your own risk.
   D. You understand that if you engage in any activities in violation of the law, including Federal, State, county or city orders, you are acting against the advice of Broker.
   E. You agree to take all reasonable and necessary precautions to protect yourself and others from the spread of COVID-19, including, but not limited to the following:
      (1) You are aware of and agree to follow all Federal, State, and local laws and orders, including Stay Home, Safer at Home, Shelter in Place orders, even though such laws and orders may be changing rapidly.
      (2) You agree and understand that it is your responsibility to exercise care to protect yourself, such as assessing your own risks, which may include age, underlying health conditions, recent travel, possible exposure to COVID-19, doctor's recommendations, local, and State and Federal recommendations.
      (3) You represent that (i) to the best of your knowledge, you are not currently afflicted with, and have not knowingly, within the last 14 days, been in contact with someone afflicted with, COVID-19, and (ii) you are not experiencing a fever, or signs of respiratory illness such as cough, shortness of breath or difficulty breathing, or other COVID-19 symptoms.
      (4) You believe that you are not likely to transmit or contract COVID-19.
      (5) When visiting or allowing someone to visit the Property, and if available, you agree to wash your hands with soap and water or use hand sanitizer, and to wear rubber gloves, a protective face mask, and protective shoe coverings. Remember to not touch your eyes, nose or mouth.
      (6) You agree to practice social distancing by keeping at least 6 feet between yourself and others. Do not gather in groups, and do not touch surfaces or items in the Property. If you believe it necessary to touch surfaces or items in the Property, consider the risks of doing so. You are reminded that wearing protective gloves, face masks, shoe coverings, and washing and sanitizing hand are steps you can take to protect yourself and others.
      (7) After showing the Property, sellers, landlords, tenants, and occupants should clean and disinfect the Property, paying attention to any areas that may be commonly touched, such as door knobs, handles, and counter tops.
      (8) After viewing the Property, visitors should discard any gloves, masks or shoe coverings worn during the visit and wash their hands with soap and water for at least twenty seconds.
5. **AGREEMENT, DECLARATION AND ASSUMPTION OF RISK:** By signing below, you are declaring the foregoing is true, that you agree to take all recommended and reasonable actions to protect yourself and others from exposure to COVID-19, and that you assume the risk, as applicable, of entering the Property, or allowing someone to enter the Property. You understand and agree that no one, including but not limited to real estate brokers and agents, can guarantee that you will not be exposed to or contract COVID-19.

By signing below, I acknowledge that I have read, understand, voluntarily agree to the foregoing, and have received a copy of this Coronavirus Property Entry Advisory and Declaration.

______________________ ______________________ Date ________
(print name) (signature)

______________________ ______________________ Date ________
(print name) (signature)

If the person signing above is a real estate licensee, complete the following:

Brokerage Company name: ______________________ DRE License # ________

Salesperson or broker-associate name: ______________________ DRE License # ________

Published and Distributed by:
REAL ESTATE BUSINESS SERVICES, LLC.
a subsidiary of the CALIFORNIA ASSOCIATION OF REALTORS®
525 South Virgil Avenue, Los Angeles, California 90020

PEAD 4/20 (PAGE 1 OF 1)

CORONAVIRUS PROPERTY ENTRY ADVISORY AND DECLARATION (PEAD PAGE 1 OF 1)

When you show up for your appointment, the rules for both agents and potential home viewers should be displayed and reviewed upon entry, with instructions regarding the usage of face coverings and hand sanitizer—these should also be made available[7].

It is required that all people entering a property, agents and brokers included, wash hands with soap and water or use hand sanitizer upon entry[7]. Note that as you view the property, your agent should be the one handling most points of contact, namely doorknobs, cabinet handles, light switches, and so on[7]. However, you may want to be overly cautious by bringing and using gloves if you plan on opening and inspecting key areas of the home.

Additionally, your agent may also open windows or doors to help circulate fresh, outside air into the space, weather permitting[7]. Properties are required to be thoroughly cleaned and disinfected before and after showings[7]. It is also advised to limit the number of people physically present at the showing and utilize social distancing techniques to help reduce the risk of potential exposure[7].

To learn more about safety protocols related to real estate transactions, check out the COVID-19 Industry Guidance: Real Estate Transactions.

WRITING OFFERS

The real estate landscape has changed so much since the introduction of COVID-19 and the aftermath that followed. While low mortgage rates have continued to fuel home-buyer demand, sellers are also not being intimidated into leaving their homes.

The industry continues to struggle with a lack of inventory, and property values continue to climb. Some sellers have taken this opportunity to capitalize on their increased equity and abandon ship but don't expect them to accept the first offer thrown at them.

In fact, due to the rising property values coupled with stiff competition, lowball offers are routinely rejected. Even on the lower end, you don't see a lot of offers for much less than 3–5% of the asking price.

Furthermore, seller tolerance has also decreased with respect to minor cosmetic requests. Asking a seller to remedy a multitude of small items will probably not get you anywhere and only delay the sales process. Similarly, sellers may be less likely to provide seller concessions or credits. However, when writing your offer, you can do a few things to differentiate your offer and set yourself up for success.

First, always include a mortgage commitment or pre-approval letter to accompany your offer. One of the biggest challenges in real estate now is financing the purchase. A pre-approval or commitment letter shows that you have already gone through the preliminary stages of securing a mortgage, and there is a stronger likelihood that you will be approved.

In many markets like the San Francisco Bay Area, to win, you need a pre-approval letter, and more often than not, an offer with no loan or appraisal contingencies. This removes the buyer's rights to back out of the offer under any circumstances.

At the same time, you need to make sure you also structure your offer to account for additional turn times. With COVID-19, some processes, such as getting a home inspection or appraisal completed, can take more time. It's important to build into your contract contingency due dates and closing flexibilities.

Lastly, ask for a home warranty to help cover the costs of repairing appliances or major home maintenance systems. Usually, sellers are pretty willing to pay the costs of a home warranty, and agents often do as well. That covers your first year of owning the home, and it can help protect you from having to pay for major unexpected repairs out-of-pocket.

SOURCES

1 Long, H. (2020, April 03). Over 10 million Americans applied for unemployment benefits in March as economy collapsed. Retrieved March 1, 2021, from https://www.washingtonpost.com/business/2020/04/02/jobless-march-coronavirus/

2 2020 Home Buyers and Sellers Generational Trends Report (Rep.). (2020, March 05). Retrieved March 1, 2021, from National Association of Realtors Research Group website: https://cdn.nar.realtor/sites/default/files/documents/2020-generational-trends-report-03-05-2020.pdf

3 Falcon, J. (2020, April 27). More home shoppers are willing to buy without seeing the property first. Retrieved March 1, 2021, from https://www.housingwire.com/articles/more-home-shoppers-are-willing-to-buy-without-seeing-the-property-first/

4 Old Republic Title. (n.d.). Digital Closing. Retrieved March 1, 2021, from https://www.oldrepublictitle.com/other-services/digital-closing

5 Richardson, B. (2020, December 15). From Curb Service To Porch Signings, Title Companies Get Creative With Social Distancing Options For Closings. Retrieved March 1, 2021, from https://www.forbes.com/sites/brendarichardson/2020/04/01/from-curb-service-to-porch-signings-title-companies-get-creative-with-social-distancing-options-for-closings/?sh=5c5f1e752192

6 California Association of Realtors. (n.d.). New Open House Guidance. Retrieved March 1, 2021, from https://www.car.org/aboutus/mediacenter/news/covidopenhouseguidance

7 California Department of Public Health, & State of California Department of Industrial Relations. (2020, July 29). COVID-19 Industry Guidance: Real Estate Transactions. Retrieved March 1, 2021, from https://files.covid19.ca.gov/pdf/guidance-real-estate.pdf

8 Fannie Mae. (2020, June 17). Appraisal Waivers - FAQs. Retrieved March 1, 2021, from https://singlefamily.fanniemae.com/media/9456/display

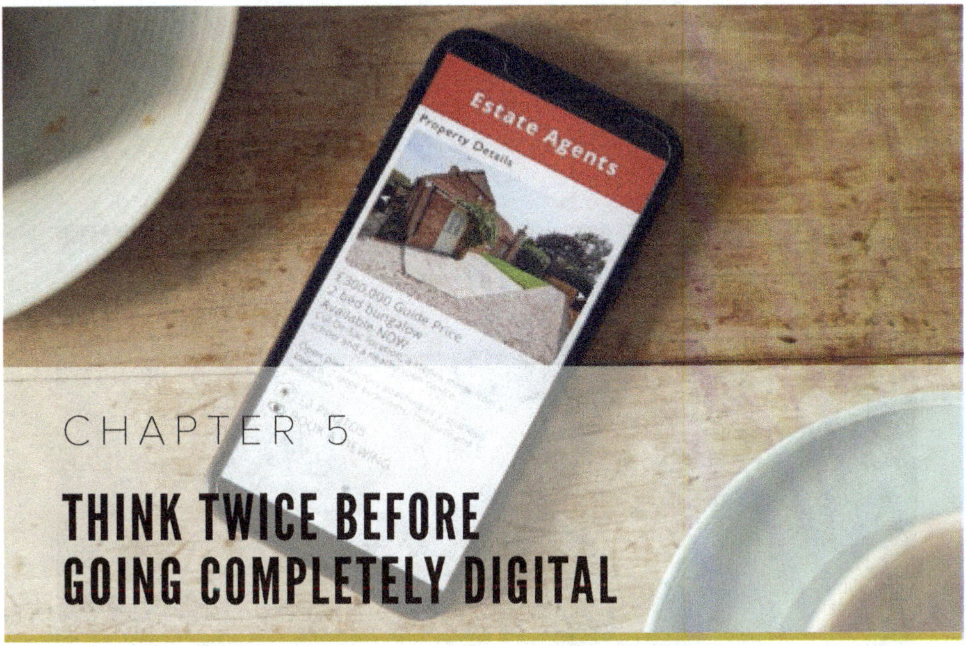

CHAPTER 5

THINK TWICE BEFORE GOING COMPLETELY DIGITAL

Experts argue that the real pivoting point in human evolution was the development and utilization of basic tools. While humanity, and society as a whole, have grown exponentially over hundreds of thousands of years, our ability to leverage both basic and complex tools has never been greater.

While we continue to use rudimentary tools (i.e., hammers, drills, saws, etc.), humans have evolved to favor electronic and digital resources. In short, you see global markets continuing to develop and adopt technologies to become more efficient and make processes easier for consumers.

The housing market is no expectation of these changes. A joint study conducted by Google and the National Association of Realtors analyzed data from the last four years and found that real-estate-related searches increased by nearly 253%1. In fact, 90% of home buyers searched online at some point during the home-buying process[1].

Consequently, these technological shifts have given rise to various online listing platforms, such as Zillow, Redfin, and NextDoor, who boast a completely digital sales experience. Buyers can now find properties online, take virtual tours, and even connect with an agent directly online.

But while it may seem like more and more buyers are turning to a completely digital home-buying process, it may shock you to learn that 88% of buyers purchase their home through a real estate agent or broker[2]. In fact, this number has been steadily increasing for almost a decade[2].

So, why are buyers utilizing individual agents over online providers? What are some of the advantages and disadvantages of using and not using an agent? Here is a closer look at why you may want to think twice before going the completely digital home-buying route.

ALL-IN-ONE ONLINE LISTING PLATFORMS

The number of online real estate listing platforms has increased dramatically over the last decade, with the initial intention of improving upon deficiencies found within the home-buying process.

Real estate is one of the oldest professions in America; however, much like other industries, it has been historically slower to adopt and incorporate new technology. Online listing platforms have tried to leverage technology to help overcome inefficiencies within the sales process while adding simplicity and value to consumers.

But in many ways, these online platforms simply build off existing data, repackage it, and provide it free to consumers. In fact, you may be losing value by going with an all-in-one online listing platform. Here are some of the key takeaways you should consider when deciding to go with a fully digital provider.

Advantages

On a macro level, one of the biggest advantages of using online listing platforms is that you can leverage the power of big data. Many platforms incorporate proprietary algorithms that analyze large data sets (often nationally, regionally, or even statewide) and use that data to churn out key metrics to add value for consumers.

For example, if you are looking to buy a new home in California, you should be able to easily pull up the total number of listings, closed sales, and average listing price (with filters to fit your search criteria) to get a good baseline for what you would need to spend on the average home in that state.

Typically, the platform itself is an advantage as most are fairly streamlined and user-friendly, making it easy to access and navigate. Easy access is an important sticking point because you can essentially run a search from anywhere you get an internet connection.

Disadvantages

While online listing platforms certainly fit within the times, as the industry is becoming more and more digital, there are several areas in which they add little to no value.

To begin with, you don't get a face with the name, meaning you often don't really know who you are working with. These platforms work all over the country, meaning you may be working with people on the back end that are in a completely different state and don't truly know your market other than the big-picture data provided to them by their system.

Similarly, when it comes to specific questions, online platforms usually do a pretty good job of answering the "what" but have trouble going deeper in answering the "why."

For example, let's say you are shopping for a new home in a particular neighborhood. The system can certainly tell you that home prices have been increasing in that area.

What it can't tell you is the reason behind why prices might be increasing. Maybe a new shopping development has brought new interest to the area. Maybe the schools are some of the best in the state. Knowing the subtle trends for local markets is really something only an agent can provide.

Lastly, online listing platforms provide little to no personalization. To the system, you are just another home buyer. It cannot really take your background and personal needs into consideration unless you give it specific parameters. Even then, you are still working with a tool, not a living person who can relate and empathize.

BUYING WITH AN AGENT

The first formal record of home sales in the United States really took off in the late 1800s, which sparked an industry of agents and brokers3. Today, the National Association of Realtors has over 1.4 million members and nearly 1,200 local associations[2].

While it may seem like real estate agents are a dime a dozen, it's important to note that no two real estate agents are the same. Each has their own process for success, and it's equally important to find an agent that is the right fit and can add extra value to your next purchase or sale.

It may seem easier to simply open your laptop and start searching for properties. Yet, there are several major advantages for buying with a traditional real estate agent rather than going strictly digital.

Advantages

One of the biggest issues with online listing platforms is that they often misdirect users by stating they can complete the entire home-buying process all online. But the truth is there are several aspects of the home-buying process that can't always be done electronically.

One example is ordering and completing general home inspections or appraisals. These are typically something that needs to be completed in person. Most platforms do not have integrations for ordering these services.

This is where a real estate agent can save you some time and headaches. You can delegate these tasks to be taken care of. Furthermore, they often have key insight into which local, reputable professionals are best for the job.

Another advantage to using a real estate agent is that you often get someone with powerhouse negotiating skills. While you can leverage data from a digital platform, it will usually be solely up to you to figure out a target price point and contingencies for your offer. By using a real estate agent, you leverage their professional experience and acumen, as well as their professional network and resources for more strategic pricing.

Lastly, using a traditional agent makes the buying process much more personalized. You don't want to work with a machine that will just treat your situation as another number or sale. Working with a live person who works and lives in the area can make buying that first home all the more satisfying. Not only that, but you also get specialized attention from an industry professional who takes the time to answer the phone and respond to your question or inquiry.

Recent data published by the National Association of Realtors found that about 91% of buyers who used an agent said they would use them again or recommend them to others[2].

Disadvantages

It's important to understand up front that not all real estate agents are the same. Many have their own processes and ways of operating their business. Some agents have also been working in real estate for several years. Others may just be starting out. The bottom line is, you may have to spend some time to find the right real estate agent for you.

Real estate agents also do not work for free. Like any other service, there is a cost to hire one. While not hiring an agent can save you a little bit of money up front, most buyers end up paying more by not hiring an agent.

Also, don't fall into the trap that going the digital route will make everything free. Online listing platforms also make money by charging clients a fee for their services, sometimes as a flat amount or as a percentage of the sales price.

SOURCES

1 The Digital House Hunt: Consumer and Market Trends in Real Estate (Rep.). (2013, March 01). Retrieved March 19, 2021, from The National Association of Realtors

website: https://www.nar.realtor/sites/default/files/documents/Study-Digital-House-Hunt-2013-01_1.pdf

2 Quick Real Estate Statistics. (2020, November 11). Retrieved March 19, 2021, from https://www.nar.realtor/research-and-statistics/quick-real-estate-statistics

3 The History of Real Estate Brokers. (2020, March 08). Retrieved March 19, 2021, from https://www.curioushistory.com/the-history-of-real-estate-brokers/

CHAPTER 6

Q1:2021, OUT OF THE FRYING PAN AND...?

Right off the bat, 2021 mirrored similar volatility experienced in the same period of 2020, as an insurrection overtook the capital when Vice President Mike Pence certified the vote count and the Biden administration secured victory. Markets had a field day speculating on what would become of the U.S. economy.

As expected, mortgage rates briefly spiked higher in mid-January, only to fall again over the next two-week period1. The rate decreases followed economic news and updates that the national economy grew slower than expected.

Both personal income and GDP growth fell short of economists' expectations, despite a decrease in consumers initiating new unemployment claims[1].

Many market experts also suspect that the vote by the House of Representatives to impeach sitting President Donald Trump on January 13 also played a key factor in the short-lived rise in rates.

The market also reacted similarly in mid-late February, close to when Donald Trump was acquitted of incitement of insurrection. Since then, markets have remained relatively stable for the quarter.

Let's take a deeper dive into how markets performed in the first quarter of 2021, what trends are becoming prevalent in housing, and discuss what the future holds for real estate for the remainder of the year and beyond.

RATES STARTING TO EXPERIENCE UPWARD PRESSURES

Heading into the new year, mortgage rates hit a record low for the start of the first quarter in 2021. The average 30-year fixed-rate mortgage dipped to around 2.65% based on data reported from aggregator Freddie Mac[2].

According to Freddie Mac, that was the lowest level it has reported in over 50 years of conducting the research survey[2]. While rates increased slightly over the next few months, they have remained stable.

During its mid-March meeting, the Federal Reserve stuck to its guns, indicating that it would continue to keep the benchmark interest rate near zero while the economy recovers3. Most experts don't expect a rate increase through 2023[3].

But rates can only stay low for so long. Keeping rates low will be dependent on how the economy recovers, and recent data already shows that pressure is starting to build. Expectations for economic growth are optimistic for the remainder of the year.

The number of mortgage loans in forbearance declining to roughly 5% of servicer portfolios coupled with decreasing new unemployment claims may be an indicator that economic activity is improving.

The U.S. GDP did grow by 6.4% for the first quarter of 2021, up from the last quarter in 2020, according to reports from the Bureau of Economic Analysis[5].

If there is a gradual uptick in rates, expect there to be a pullback on mortgage refinances. Refinance volume already started to decline toward the end of the quarter, with applications trending back to favoring purchases.

Ending the week of March 19, purchases increased by roughly 3% on both an adjusted and unadjusted basis[4]. Industry professionals cite borrowers seeking more room to stretch their legs and demand for home ownership within young families as driving factors to the increase[4].

OVERBIDDING TREND ESCALATES

It's no surprise that home prices pulled higher over 2020, creating a barrier of entry for many new prospective home buyers.

In the first quarter of 2021 alone, home prices on existing single-family homes rose at a rate of 16.2%[8]. That's the highest since 1989, with all metro areas experiencing double-digit growth[8].

In March, the median home price in the U.S. was just shy of $275,000[9]. But rising home prices are not the only reason new homebuyers can't land a deal.

A recent survey by Redfin found that 56% of all buyers experienced a bidding war in January, meaning that unaffordable prices are only one obstacle buyers must overcome[6].

The combination of increased competition and lack of inventory leads to homes closing at record rates. Data suggests homes are quickly going under contract within two weeks, whereas under standard market conditions, it could take anywhere from 4 to 12 weeks before buyers would have an accepted offer[6].

Similarly, housing saw one of the most significant declines in inventory, citing a 25.7% decrease in year-over-year numbers based on metrics from the National Association of Realtors[7].

A BATTLE BETWEEN INFLATION AND LIQUIDITY

When the pandemic first became relevant and the CARES Act was passed to allow for broad-spectrum relief to borrowers with government-owned mortgages, mortgage servicers experienced a liquidity crisis.

As we mentioned, to ensure that housing and mortgage markets remained solvent, the Federal Reserve committed to purchasing mortgage-backed securities while also dropping the benchmark interest rate to near zero.

The problem is that at some point, the Federal Reserve will cease purchasing mortgage-backed securities at the current rate. If there is another liquidity breakdown, it could decrease consumer confidence and further impact financial markets.

By the end of March, the Federal Reserve held roughly $2.2 trillion in agency mortgage-backed securities.

In theory, slowing MBS purchase activity could help cool the housing market and retract home prices, but this could be a bigger issue when you factor in inflation.

Not many people realize the role inflation plays in the market and its impact on home buying. As prices for goods and services continue to climb, the dollar loses purchasing power over time.

Shelter is no exception. If inflation continues to rise, the central bank will most likely continue its purchasing of mortgage-backed securities until inflation falls in line at an appropriate level.

Unfortunately, the lack of inventory may only be exacerbating the cyclical issue. Keep in mind that inventory shortages don't just impact new home buyers.

Existing sellers looking to buy, upgrade to a bigger home, or relocate, may also find competition discouraging, which would mean them staying in their existing home longer and not listing it.

What's worse is that the increasing cost to build also creates added pressure, making it hard to add new homes to the market. For example, lumber prices have tripled over the last 12 months, according to the National Association of Homebuilders[10].

Lower mortgage rates are great but finding a home that has all your desired features in a market with limited supply while saving up for a down payment as home prices continue to climb would be challenging for anyone.

KEY TAKEAWAYS

The first part of 2021 started out with similar issues as 2020, with the exception that the national economy now has had a year of dealing with a modern pandemic. Although trepidatious, the economy has shown signs of recovery.

Mortgage rates continue to remain at or near record lows, and GDP is finally showing signs of expansion. Even the number of mortgages in forbearance and new unemployment claims have decreased.

However, as the economy continues to recover, more pressure will be placed on the Federal Reserve to increase interest rates. This also comes coupled with a cry from consumers to help cool home prices.

Home prices and rampant competition are creating barriers for new home buyers looking to enter the market. Bidding wars are becoming more and more prevalent, and while homebuilders are trying to inject new inventory into the market, prices for materials and labor seem also to be an issue with no distinct resolution in sight.

For now, new buyers will have to continue to tread water and fight for those properties that are available in the market or consider exiting the market until prices begin to taper off.

One sign of relief is the Federal Reserve's willingness to increase rates if the economy as a whole continues to show signs of expansion. Hopefully, the economy can continue this momentum in the foreseeable future.

SOURCES

1 Campisi, N. (2021, January 28). Today's Mortgage Interest Rates: Jan. 28, 2021-Mortgage Rates Fall As The Economy Hibernates.

Retrieved May 24, 2021, from https://www.forbes.com/advisor/mortgages/mortgage-interest-rates-01-28-2021/

2 Bahney, A. (2021, January 07). Mortgage rates kick off 2021 with a new record low. Retrieved May 24, 2021, from https://www.cnn.com/2021/01/07/success/mortgage-rates-fall-january/index.html

3 Reinicke, C. (2021, March 17). Heres how the Fed decision impacts your wallet. Retrieved May 24, 2021, from https://www.cnbc.com/2021/03/17/how-the-fed-decision-to-keep-interest-rates-low-impacts-your-wallet.html#:~:text=The Federal Reserve on Wednesday kept its benchmark interest rate,recovery from the coronavirus pandemic.&text=That means that historic low,hike is unlikely through 2023.

4 Swanson, J. (2021, March 24). Purchase Application Volume up for Fourth Consecutive Week. Retrieved

May 24, 2021, from http://www.mortgagenewsdaily.com/03242021_applications_and_forbearances.asp

5 Bureau of Economic Analysis, U.S. Department of Commerce. (2021, April 29). Gross Domestic Product, First Quarter 2021 (Advance Estimate) [Press release]. Retrieved May 24, 2021, from https://www.bea.gov/sites/default/files/2021-04/gdp1q21_adv.pdf

6 Olick, D. (2021, February 13). Bidding wars are off the charts, as home listings fall to a record low. Retrieved May 24, 2021, from https://www.cnbc.com/2021/02/12/bidding-wars-for-homes-are-off-the-charts-as-listings-fall-to-record-low.html

7 Campisi, N. (2021, February 25). Today's Mortgage Interest Rates: Mortgage Rates, New Home Sales Shoot Up. Retrieved May 24, 2021, from https://www.forbes.com/advisor/mortgages/mortgage-interest-rates-02-25-2021/

8 Simmons, Q. (2021, May 11). Virtually Every Metro Area Experienced Home Prices Rise in First Quarter of 2021. Retrieved May 24, 2021, from https://www.nar.realtor/newsroom/virtually-every-metro-area-experienced-home-prices-rise-in-first-quarter-of-2021

9 Businesswire. (2021, April 22). ADDING MULTIMEDIA U.S. Home Prices End First Quarter on Very Strong Note, Radian Home Price Index Reveals. Retrieved May 24, 2021, from https://www.businesswire.com/news/home/20210422005503/en/ADDING-MULTIMEDIA-U.S.-Home-Prices-End-First-Quarter-on-Very-Strong-Note-Radian-Home-Price-Index-Reveals

CHAPTER 7

MOVING ON...A REVIEW OF Q2 2021, MARKET DATA, AND INDUSTRY INSIGHTS

While the country is now past many of the political and economic pressures that escalated in the earlier part of the first quarter of 2021, the economy isn't out of the woods just yet.

As analysts predicted, the recovery slowly gained traction in the summer months as businesses reopened and people returned to work.

In fact, the unemployment rate declined by about 0.5% to 5.4% as measured in July according to the U.S. Bureau of Labor Statistics[1]. Similarly, median family incomes rose to a little over $58,000 compared to around $51,000 in the previous quarter[2].

Comparatively, while other industries are taking the slow and steady approach, housing continues its rapid expansion, showing little signs of deceleration.

Mortgage interest rates continue to remain near all-time record lows, with the average U.S. 30-year fixed-rate mortgage rate dropping to approximately 3.05% in the second quarter[2].

This is nearly a 0.25% decrease from the same period the previous year[2]. While not a huge drop, low rates are helping drive growth as refinance activity has started to cool.

Despite the market facing some upward pressure as the Federal Reserve announced its plan to taper the purchasing of mortgage-backed securities as early as the third quarter, purchase activity has remained strong[3].

All signs point to a strong and stable housing market. But what future opportunities can industry professionals, home buyers, and investors alike expect heading into the last half of the year?

Will the market continue a stable trajectory, or will other headwinds impede growth? How will the Delta variant impact housing on a macro level?

Let's take a closer look at how well markets have fared, what trends and changes have arisen since the first quarter, and what you should expect to see coming down the pipeline in the not-so-distant future.

PULLBACK ON COVID-19-RELATED OVERLAYS?

One of the most significant factors in helping keep markets stable when COVID-19 was first introduced was that lenders tightened down on credit requirements. Some lenders even moved away from riskier loan programs in favor of those backed by the federal government.

But receding exposure was not the only outcome brought about by the pandemic. Aggregators Fannie Mae and Freddie Mac both announced enhanced COVID-19 appraisal flexibilities and underwriting guidelines that required additional due diligence when qualifying borrowers for a new mortgage.

For example, self-employed borrowers now had to provide proof the business was open and operating, as well as supply additional financial data regarding the solvency of the business, including, but not limited to, year-to-date profit and loss statements and business bank statements.

While these COVID-19-specific overlays helped increase loan quality and mitigate additional risks in the market, they also made it hard for borrowers to qualify. However, as the economy recovered, the need for these additional overlays has been called into question.

Optimistically, Fannie Mae and Freddie Mac have both retired specific COVID-19 appraisal flexibilities. While desktop or exterior-only appraisals may have been permitted in certain circumstances, all applications taken after May 31, 2021, that require an appraisal will have to follow the pre-pandemic guidelines[4].

This action could be interpreted that borrowers, investors, and industry professionals alike should be confident in the trajectory of this economic recovery. But remaining optimistic doesn't mean people shouldn't err on the side of caution.

The impending Delta variant could certainly shift housing trends in a negative direction. Not only could the variant impact the economy as a whole, subsequently having a negative impact on interest rates, but it could also smother existing home owners and thereby exacerbate the ongoing inventory shortage, which has caused barriers to entry for many new home buyers.

Nevertheless, the pullback on COVID-19-related overlays should help increase turn times and improve credit availability in the interim. The Mortgage Bankers Association (MBA) noted that productivity increased to 3.7 loans originated per production employee per month compared to 3.6 loans in the first quarter[5].

FANNIE MAE LAUNCHES REFINOW PROGRAM IN JUNE

Coming in at the perfect time, just as refinance activity has started to diminish, Fannie Mae launched its new RefiNow program in June 2021 to help borrowers with Fannie-Mae-backed loans who could benefit from the lower rate environment but may not be able to afford the upfront costs involved with refinancing[6].

The main purpose of the program is to help qualifying home owners reduce their monthly housing costs and save money. Freddie Mac has also announced a similar program, dubbed Refi Possible, but has yet to be made available to borrowers.

To qualify as a RefiNow mortgage, borrowers must see a reduction in their interest rate by at least 50 basis points, as well as a reduction in their monthly payment by at least $50[6]. Note that this program cannot be combined with other affordable housing programs such as Fannie Mae's HomeReady program[6].

In general, the new loan must have a fixed interest rate, be a limited cash-out refinance, and be secured by a 1-unit primary residence[6]. One positive factor is that DTI restrictions are much more liberal with this program, meaning more borrowers should qualify.

The maximum DTI ratio is currently capped at 65%[6]. Other programs' specific guidelines also apply, and borrowers must also meet income eligibility requirements.

It's not certain if RefiNow will go away as COVID-19 becomes less prevalent; however, it does address many growing concerns in the market.

One of the more meaningful expectations is that the program should help distressed borrowers who may need additional relief as government assistance programs begin to dry up. It should also help slow the weakening demand for refinances, which has many lenders concerned about profit margins.

THE FIRST-TIME HOME BUYER ACT ANNOUNCED

Inventory remained one of the biggest obstacles for first-time home buyers in the second quarter of 2021. While the number of homes listed for sale increased nationally by 5.5% compared to the prior year, home prices also followed suit[7].

In June, prices grew by nearly 13%, with 94% of markets showing double-digit home price appreciation[2]. Nationally, the median home price hit $357,900, with 54% of homes selling above listing price[2].

Thankfully, relief regarding home affordability may be on the way, according to new legislation introduced to Congress.

In late April, President Joe Biden introduced a bill now referred to as the First-Time Homebuyer Act geared toward making home-buying more affordable for American consumers[8].

The bill proposes providing eligible first-time home buyers with a tax credit equal to 10% of the purchase price of a new home or $15,000, whichever is less[8].

Eligible borrowers cannot have owned or purchased a home within the last three years and must live in the home for at least four years[8]. Income restrictions may apply.

The bill still must go through several steps before it becomes written into law. There is heavy criticism of the need for this tax credit, although there is a precedent for past first-time home-buyer tax credits.

The Housing and Economic Recovery Act of 2008 created a similar tax credit for first-time home buyers, although on a much smaller scale[8].

If this legislation passes, it could help bolster purchase activity and help retain the momentum seen in the market over the last year.

KEY TAKEAWAYS

The market is showing signs of normalization compared to the previous quarter. The national economy seems to be slowly recovering as several metrics show a positive uptick.

Housing and mortgage markets continue to expand as rates remain reasonably low for the foreseeable future, although affordability continues to be the main issue facing home buyers today.

While bidding wars are becoming a lot less prevalent, home prices continue to climb. Buyers may find new headwinds if the Delta variant starts to cause additional economic turmoil, thereby prolonging this economic recovery.

However, the silver lining is that lenders are now focusing their attention on purchase originations rather than refinances, as refinance activity has declined tremendously. This has also led to more favorable turn times.

Furthermore, buyers should be optimistic that agencies are now moving away from COVID-19-related credit requirements while simultaneously creating new mortgage programs and incentives that may soon make home ownership easier.

SOURCES

1 Bureau of Labor Statistics, U.S. Department of Labor. (2021, August 6). The Employment Situation - July 2021 [Press release]. Retrieved August 27, 2021, from https://www.bls.gov/news.release/pdf/empsit.pdf

2 Hyman, M. (2021, August 12). Single-Family Home Prices Rose in 99% of 183 Metro Areas in 2021 Q2. Retrieved August 27, 2021, from https://www.nar.realtor/blogs/economists-outlook/single-family-home-prices-rose-in-99-of-183-metro-areas-in-2021-q2

3 Dan Burns, A. S. (2021, June 11). Fed may opt for faster phase-out of housing-backed bond purchases. Retrieved August 27, 2021, from https://www.reuters.com/business/fed-may-opt-faster-phase-out-housing-backed-bond-purchases-2021-06-11/

4 Fannie Mae. (2021, April 21). Lender Letter (LL-2021-04) All Fannie Mae Single-Family Sellers Impact of COVID-19 on Appraisals [Press release]. Retrieved August 27, 2021, from https://singlefamily.fanniemae.com/media/24816/display

5 DeSanctis, A. (2021, August 24). IMB Production Profits Decline in Second Quarter of 2021: Mortgage Bankers Association. Retrieved August 27, 2021, from https://www.mba.org/2021-press-releases/august/imb-production-profits-decline-in-second-quarter-of-2021

6 Fannie Mae. (2021). RefiNow Product Matrix [Brochure]. Author. Retrieved August 27, 2021, from https://singlefamily.fanniemae.com/media/25951/display

7 Speianu, S., & Hale, D. (2021, June 30). June 2021 Housing Market Trends Report - Realtor.com Research. Retrieved August 27, 2021, from https://www.realtor.com/research/june-2021-data/

8 Freddie Mac. (2021, July 21). Quarterly Research Package and Forecast: Q2 2021. Retrieved August 27, 2021, from https://crt.freddiemac.com/news-insights/reports-research/quarterly-research-package-and-forecast-q2-2021

CHAPTER 8

SO... WHEN IS THE BEST TIME TO BUY A NEW HOME?

Buying a new home is a big decision that should not be taken lightly. New home buyers often forget that a home is a long-term investment, which can take a lot of time and money to maintain.

Even if you are a veteran real estate investor or a seasoned home owner looking to upgrade or relocate to a new dwelling, buying a new home is still a major commitment.

Studies do show that there are numerous advantages to buying versus renting your own residence, but it's important to consider all the factors involved with owning before you make the leap to being a home owner.

While splashy headlines and news articles boast a robust housing market with near-record-low interest rates, the truth is that you shouldn't buy a home until it makes sense for you. Market conditions aside, some people may be better off renting or are simply not ready for home ownership.

If you have been thinking about buying a new home but have been on the fence about when the best time to buy might be, here are a few factors to consider that may help you decide when to pull the trigger.

CAN YOU AFFORD A NEW HOUSE?

One of the overarching factors that you need to figure out before you purchase a new home is whether you can afford it or not. The biggest obstacles impacting new home buyers today are all debt-related, making it harder to save for a down payment.

A recent survey by the National Association of Realtors found that 51% of home buyers found student loans to be the biggest hurdle impacting their savings, compared to 45% who mention credit card debt, and 38% that found card loans to be the most burdening[1].

Assuming the down payment isn't an issue, the next thing to consider is your monthly payment. If you are currently renting and looking to transition to home ownership, it seems easy just to compare a typical mortgage payment and match it up to your current monthly rent payment.

But there are a lot more costs involved with buying a home than just a principal and interest payment. For example, when you rent (except for renters' insurance), you are not typically responsible for any other expenses associated with living in the property.

However, as a home owner, you have to factor in property taxes, home owner's insurance coverage, and any home owner's association dues (if applicable) into your monthly budget.

Also, consider any monthly mortgage insurance premiums. Most lenders will typically allow you to borrow up to 95% of what your home is worth. But what they don't tell you is that if you put less than 20% down, you will be paying for private mortgage insurance.

Finally, don't forget your monthly utilities. While some rentals do charge tenants for certain utility costs associated with living in the property, this is not always the case. Utility costs add up, so make sure to consider their impact on your overall budget.

A good rule of thumb for determining how much home you can afford is by calculating your total net pay (take-home pay) each month and ensuring any new housing payment (all costs included) does not exceed 25% of that total.

Many new home buyers use free affordability calculators. An affordability calculator will take your data inputs about your monthly budget and spit out a range of what your typical budget could afford.

Better calculators will tell you what homes you can afford at different price points to help you determine if you will be stretching your budget too thin or if you can comfortably afford the new proposed housing payment.

WHAT IS THE MARKET DOING?

The best time to buy a new home is whenever it feels right to you. However, it's always a good idea to stay informed on market trends, which could help influence your buying decision.

If you are a new home buyer, it may be tricky to time the market looking for a deal. In fact, with rising home prices and a lack of available homes for sale, competition is making it harder for buyers to snag anything below the asking price.

While price is a major factor, you should also check how mortgage interest rates are performing. Lower mortgage interest rates are more favorable to buyers because not only will you pay less in interest over time, but you can also increase your buying power.

Mortgage rates are currently near record lows. January 2021 marked the 17th time rates hit historic lows over a 12-month period[5]. At that point, the average U.S. 30-year fixed-rate mortgage was 2.65%[5].

Recent reports also indicate that Millennials, Generation Y, and Generation X currently make up the biggest share of home buyers at 61%[3]. Out of all buyers, 31% were first-time home buyers[3].

More and more people are looking to buy, with Millennials taking up most of the market share. While market conditions may seem crazy at times, find comfort knowing you are not the only one looking to buy your first home.

Similarly, understand that real estate has been traditionally slower to adopt new processes and technologies. However, thanks to COVID-19, industry professionals have had to evolve and adopt new digital solutions to meet the changing environment. This may change the way you buy real estate now and in the future.

Considering the future, if you are invested in buying a new home, it's good to factor in how long you intend to live in the home. There are a lot of upfront costs associated with getting a home—both time and money. It may not be worth going through the home-buying process only to move a short time after.

Ultimately, buying a home is a long-term investment. With that, it can appreciate over time if you take care of it. Recent data suggest that annual price growth over the last 25 years has been roughly 4%[2].

However, in September of 2020, home prices increased upwards of 14%, which was one of the most significant increases over the last few decades[2]. Home prices have continued to rise for various reasons, but the point is that real estate typically goes up in value over time. Make sure you factor this into your buying decision.

ARE YOU PREPARED FOR THE UPKEEP?

One of the biggest things new buyers forget to factor into their buying decision is if they are prepared to handle inevitable home maintenance projects that come with owning a home.

Like other tangible assets, houses deteriorate over time. If you want your home to retain (or increase) its value while being a safe and comfortable place to live, it may involve a little bit of elbow grease.

In 2018, most home owners spent an average of $1,105 on home maintenance and completed an average of 7 home maintenance projects. If you were renting, a landlord would typically cover these repairs. But when you become a home owner, upkeep costs come directly out of your pocket.

To put it in perspective, HomeAdvisor found that the national average to replace plumbing cost roughly $350 to $2,000, depending on the size of the project. Replacing a roof will run you anywhere from $5,000 to $10,000 or more. Lastly, the average cost of electrical wiring replacement and installation is between $550 and $2,200.

Clearly, home maintenance and improvements do not come cheap. Make sure you are prepared to cover these related expenses before you purchase that new dream home.

Thank you so much for reading this book, and I wish you the best in your real estate ventures!

SOURCES

1 2020 Downpayment Expectations & Hurdles to Homeownership (Rep.). (2020, April). Retrieved June 1, 2021, from National Association of Realtors Research Group website: https://www.nar.realtor/sites/default/files/documents/2020-downpayment-expectations-and-hurdles-to-homeownership-report-04-16-2020.pdf

2 Rudy, M. (2021, February 24). America's House Price History: Does Homeownership Still Pay Off? Retrieved June 1, 2021, from https://www.homelight.com/blog/house-price-history/

3 2021 Home Buyers and Sellers Generational Trends Report (Rep.). (2021, March 16). Retrieved June 1, 2021, from National Association of Realtors Research Group website: https://www.nar.realtor/sites/default/files/documents/2021-home-buyers-and-sellers-generational-trends-03-16-2021.pdf

4 State of Home Spending 2019 (Rep.). (n.d.). Retrieved June 1, 2021, from HomeAdvisor website: https://www.homeadvisor.com/r/wp-content/uploads/2019/06/StateOfHomeSpending2019.pdf

5 Orton, K. (2021, January 07). Fixed mortgage rates sink to lowest levels in history but could be headed higher. Retrieved June 1, 2021, from https://www.washingtonpost.com/business/2021/01/07/fixed-mortgage-rates-sink-lowest-levels-history-could-be-headed-higher/

ABOUT THE AUTHOR

Garrick Werdmuller entered the mortgage business in 2002. After Garrick graduated from the California Culinary Academy and worked his way up to sous chef at the Hyatt Regency Embarcadero in San Francisco, 9/11 hit. Garrick was laid off almost immediately as catering events got canceled one after the other. Tired of working long hours and making money for other people while struggling to earn a living in San Francisco, Garrick talked to a friend who didn't seem to have the problems he did. His friend was a loan officer.

It was that day he ordered his Principles of Real Estate class, and the rest is history. Garrick started in the business cold-calling potential refinance prospects off data lists, and the people he spoke with really liked him, trusted him, and needed his help. Right away, Garrick discovered how important a mortgage expert could be in people's lives.

Made in the USA
Monee, IL
03 November 2026

67387903R00049